# Terminal Destination

Poems by

## Cameron Morse

Spartan Press
Kansas City, MO
spartanpresskc.com

Copyright © Cameron Morse, 2019
First Edition 1 3 5 7 9 10 8 6 4 2
ISBN: 978-1-950380-46-6
LCCN: 2019943983

Design, edits and layout: Jason Ryberg
Cover and title page image: Li Ni
Author photo: Brian Compton
All rights reserved. No part of this publication may be reproduced or transmitted in any form or by any means, electronic or mechanical, including photocopying, recording or by info retrieval system, without prior written permission from the author.

Acknowledgments:

I am grateful to my wife Lili and my son Theodore. Our adventures together are the inspiration for these poems. I thank my parents for taking me with them to China and China for doing the rest. I am also grateful to members of the GBM SURVIVORS TO THIVERS! Facebook group for their stories; Jason Ryberg, for welcoming me into the Spartan family; Jordan Stempleman, for lending a helping ear; the Creative Writing Program at the University of Missouri—Kansas City and the editors in whose magazines the following poems first appeared (some in earlier forms):

*2River View:* "Trespassing." *Aeolian Harp Anthology:* "Dog Water." *Algebra of Owls:* "KFC Rhapsody." *Art of Nursing:* "Infant Colonoscopy." *Braided Way:* "Preliminary Investigations." *Cha: An Asian Literary Journal:* "Elegy for Ni Yilin." *Coldnoon:* "Terminal Destination." *Edify Fiction:* "Tunnels." *Flint Hills Review:* "Looking at the Courtyard." *The Healing Muse:* "Chemo Baby." *LETTERS Journal* : "Give Thanks." *Lines + Stars:* "Landscape Fabric." *Mizmor Anthology 2019 Poetry Collection:* "The Long Flight Out of Myself." *October Hill Magazine:* "Night Trains." *Oddball Magazine:* "Household Idol." *The Opiate:* "Carrot Cake." *Oyster River Pages:* "Mother-in-Law." *Pirene's Fountain:* "Orchid Garden Residence Community," "The Names of Children," "Offerings." *Rumble Fish Quarterly:* "Orange Lions." *San Pedro River Review:* "Massage Parlor." *Sou'wester:* "Akimbo." *Spillway: A Poetry Magazine:* "Security Guards." *Steam Ticket:* "Etoposide." *Straylight Literary Magazine:* "Berlin." *Sweet Tree Review:* "Two Pronged Attack," "Travel Plans," "First Day in Beijing," "Last Flight Before the Burial." *THAT Literary Review:* "Garage Sale in the Rain." *Tar River Poetry:* "Raking Leaves." *Touchstone:* "Self-Portrait in an MRI Machine." *Vita Brevis:* "In Search of Cherry Blossoms." *West Trade Review:* "Terminal Diagnosis."

# TABLE OF CONTENTS

Elegy for Ni Yilin / 1

*domestic*

Infant Colonoscopy / 7

Chemo Baby / 8

Landscape Fabric / 9

Etoposide / 11

Preliminary Investigations / 12

Garage Sale in the Rain / 13

Berlin / 14

Raking Leaves / 16

Akimbo / 17

Two-Pronged Attack / 18

Give Thanks / 20

Dog Water / 21

Trespassing / 22

Terminal Diagnosis / 23

Orange Lions / 25

Carrot Cake / 26

Self-Portrait in an MRI Machine / 27

Travel Plans / 28

*international*

The Long Flight Out of Myself / 30

First Day in Beijing / 32

Security Guards / 33

Orchid Garden Residence Community / 34

KFC Rhapsody / 36

Last Flight Before the Burial / 38

Tunnels / 39

Co-Sleeping / 40

Looking at the Courtyard / 41

The Names of Children / 42

Mother-in-Law / 44

After the Revolution / 46

Food Fight / 47

Night Trains / 49

Massage Parlor / 50

Household Idol / 52

In Search of Cherry Blossoms / 53

Offerings / 54

Visiting the Tomb / 56

What Time Does / 57

Morning Departure / 58

Terminal Destination / 60

*for my family*

# TERMINAL DESTINATION

# Elegy for Ni Yilin

*Nov. 18, 2016*

My father-in-law would wait
in the train station's maelstrom
of human body parts and odors
to take my hand like a child's.

Sidle up on the sofa, slurring
in his local dialect of love.
In the letterbox of thumb
and forefinger, forefinger and thumb,

Yilin framed mountains in negligees
of mist, listened to Beethoven
on a DVD player. From my first visit,
I remember the hospital courtyard
with its one chopped pollard,
boulders rearing like elephant
ghosts among the high rises.

A medicine doctor rolled eggs
over the bulge of his pleural sac,
his eyeballs yellowed like rice
paper in the province of his birth.
Yilin hallucinated bats, a flight
of stairs, a sealed envelope.

On the first anniversary of his death,
his daughter crosses the chicken wire
fence to snip a sprig of garden mint
and garnish the fish after his recipe.

She remembers the carp he carried
home, still beating in a clear bag
of water, how he held the blade
of its body in both hands, to check
the flex, the smile of its spine.

She remembers her girlhood,
bumblebees philandering in fields
of rapeseed, riders in the border
between shadow and light,
how balcony tile glittered with silver
scales, coins in the currency
of life and death, headstones
terraced between today
and tomorrow.

Yilin began to learn the language
of the dead when the forehead
of his infant son forged fire,
then frosted over. It didn't make him
flinch to swipe the neck
of a chicken or jam his thumb
between the lips of the fish.

How else would it be possible
to live? His old man knocked
on the wrong door and thought
his own son unwilling to open.

I remember the doctors talking
stomach pipe, their ultimatum:
One more drink, and you're dead.

*domestic*

## Infant Colonoscopy

Nurses billow in yellow gowns around my baby boy.
Surgical masks catch their breaths.
Visors intervene between dry eyes and our octagonal room
at Children's Mercy where Glow-In-The-Dark
Stars plucked off the dark blue wall constellate white chips
of sheetrock. All around the ready room,
families in separate partitions gather around children
who are about to go under. If the biopsy site
bleeds, explains the anesthesiologist, we will have to cauterize
or clip. If we tear an intestine,
he'll have to go into emergency surgery.
Ushered out, Lili and I catch one last glance of him
looking for us, his neck stretched
like a turtle's over the shoulder of a complete stranger.

## Chemo Baby

Might not want to rush
into that, your radiologist says, late
evening light casting the dark
shape of your house over the side yard.

My year-old Theo runs barefoot
across the cracked driveway, turns and patters
back calling *da-dee!* Sparrows chirrup
atop the sunset-crested yew, golden

in the glare. They say as the world ends,
we enter the throes of a sixth mass extinction.
Rumor dogears my knockoff
Moleskine. Theo scoots down the piebald slope,

reverses and crawls back up.
Maybe the last light is one we clutch
to the chest, the one that falls
askance. Theo steps to the gritty edge

of the driveway, stalls at the precipice.
With fear and trembling, my wife
and I conceived him. Our cryobank destroyed
my uncontaminated specimen.

# Landscape Fabric

What have I come for
if not some news of you, old
neighbor who moved away,
my ancient of days? Every day
I come to the same place
and wait. I sit with a traffic of tiny
ants swerving to-and-fro
in the sidewalk crack, the stroller
parked at the garage door.
I wait with the empty watering
can, the landscape fabric's
torn end put out like a tongue
in pea gravel. It's the torn end
I cling to, the tattered lip
of black plastic that sits up
and lies down at the wind's request.

## Etoposide

I peel the banana from the bottom
the way monkeys do, parsing
the stringy tusk into bite-sized chunks.

When you cock your neck in the booster seat
and mew in mimicry of Sherlock, the cockapoo
on the back patio, who whines

because he knows we are going to let him
in soon to mop up your droppings,
we know it's time to break out the banana.

I don't eat bananas.
I don't even lick my fingers
after handling yours. Somewhere in Anaheim,

a girl called Giselle who has the same kind
of cancer I do is going on etoposide
because her guerrilla cells have crossed the blood-brain barrier

and infiltrated her spine, which explains why
she has a hard time walking to the bathroom, why she slurs
her words, dresses up as a zombie for Halloween,

and gets to go to Disney World for free,
but not the feeling I get at the butcher block, looking
down at the blue vein in your temple, your cheeks

ballooning with banana. Why when I draw breath
is it spring again in Golden Acres, am I small
again and filled with birdsong?

## Preliminary Investigations

A red spider tick charges
over the blank hill

of my ankle. In the grass,
my socks prickle.

Blades swing like needles
on a scale that weighs

the wind. My elbow itches.
When a young ladybug

walks the promenade
of my armrest, I am

no longer the poet. I am
the landscape.

Garage Sale in the Rain


Beyond the door on tracks above us, rain falls
like white rice, graining dark trunks
across the cul-de-sac.

Nevertheless, they come.
Bargain shoppers and bored retirees follow
the signs to our dimly lit cement enclosure of folding tables.

Sequins of rain drape stings over the broken back
of the driveway they pilgrim—the cracked,
keeling blocks of pavement accepting payment for the sky's

transgressions. An old navy man presses his hand
between the chill blades of the oil-filled
radiator, waiting for warmth,

for the promised heat to sear him. It doesn't,
not fast enough anyway,
but in the next interval of stillness, breezes shake loose

a patter of raindrops from the pin oak,
and a large woman with Botoxed lips leaves with it
wrapped in a blanket.

## Berlin

When I want to go on to Polar Bear Passage
while you peruse the giftshop,
you see through my request. Always going off
to be alone with my writing, double up
and live twice, once with you,
once with my imaginary friends, my invisible
audience, but then you dream I died again
and wake up sobbing because you say
you don't know how to live without me
and I realize you're just like Berlin, the polar bear
pacing her cement platform, glorified
parking lot painted white in cheap imitation
of snow and it's burning her paws because it's July
in Missouri and the Arctic is so far away.

## Raking Leaves

I want to comb the leaves
out of the green hair of my lawn,

brush out the clumps of oak and maple,
stalks of hay from the clipped bale,

the stuffed dog house.
If one of us must work in the dark

corner, the crux where pickets meet
and shadows converse,

let it be me. I love the moss
that cushions the severed roots

of yesteryear. I would peel back
the dank bandage of matted

catkins, smooth the poultice of mud,
air out the wounds

that want for lack of sun.
While my little brother chases tatters

back and forth across the sky,
leaf blower shrieking in his hands,

I would unearth ice-encrusted dog
turds and burst acorns, allow

the strokes of my tiny green rake
to become as rhythmic as story,

repetitive as mantra, sink into the cadence
and lose myself in the work.

# Akimbo

After Lili weans him off the breast,
Theo switches to a bottle, then a sippy cup.
After the privacy fence goes up,

the shadow wing harbors semi-permanent snow.
Ice hardens where the chain links once cast a latticework
of light. After a period of time,

her period returns. I find a blood-stiffened pair
of panties in the laundry room and rinse. There's a secret
that I'm in on. There's a study on the evolving

role of cannabis therapy in glioblastoma treatment.
One baby born, the other becomes a topic
for discussion. One participant dead,

the student asks what may be concluded. One knee akimbo,
the other outstretched, one arm flung overhead,
the other holds him to her creased breast.

## Two-Pronged Attack

Freight trains woo, woo like some sort of haunted
mansion, a sheet of cloud the sky wears
over its head. I find a droplet

of blood on the toilet seat. Theodore rummages
in the oak-leafed flowerbed for a cobwebbed
bird house. There is the fact of chicken-scratched

coffee table marquetry, a constellation of pock marks
below my hand. I feel the damage.
There is grit, clots of tangled hair and lint

emptied from the vacuum cleaner.
Knitting circle loose configurations of geese
break over the house, honking.

The cancer kids in my dream are music students
unlikely to qualify for a grant, explains
my oncologist, because they have what I have.

From the kitchen I saw him standing
at the forbidden drawer for the hundredth time.
Neglected to wrest away his tiny hand.

Afterwards, I discovered the adapter and removed it.
The question of guilt is I represent the accused.
I could have intervened.

## Give Thanks

Give thanks, green buds
for your hard fuzzy nipples

in the leafless tines
of the magnolia sapling.

Wobble in the shushings,
the sibilants of November breeze

and give thanks.
Among the dogs at noontime,

I would like nothing
better than to close my eyes

in sunlight, feet up on the rim
of the firepit, and let my body

beckon. Let the sunbeaten
side of my head call to the shaded

hemisphere, praise and give
thanks for its ghost.

I would like to take
my cue from the cockapoo.

Roll around in crispy leaves,
lie with my incisive shadow

brother in a fountainhead
of yellow sleep.

# Dog Water

I slam down the frozen bowl
in the backyard's palisade of shadow and ice.

My father-in-law is finally, finally to be buried
same time, next month.

Nestlings chirrup in the bird house: house sparrows;
somewhere, a crow says *Cameron*.

Snow dust collects in the scalloped rim of the bird
bath, its shell troughs of cement.

I slam down the white disc of dog water. For four years,
Yilin's been waiting to be buried.

I know if I let this block of ice alone, it will sit here
until the first thaw in this statuary of ice

and shadow. My Chinese is so rusty
I'm afraid to say hello.

## Trespassing

Stray with me. Fasten and fixate.
A wagon wheel leans against the pickets.

Go, investigate,
investigate the flowerbed, the basketball goals

and extension ladders lying on their sides.
These summer houses are mostly empty in December,

these gascans, iceboxes,
leftover pelts of snow on unraked riverside lawns.

It's unlikely that you will remember this,
how you stumbled among the rusty boat trailers

in the pre-dawn where I don my coveralls.
It's unlikely you will remember me at all.

What does the water have to say?
What does the light have to say to the water?

And you, would you please just call me Daddy?
I know you know some words.

It's just us out here on the rock bank of the Mississippi.
Let me lean over. Whisper something in my ear.

## Terminal Diagnosis

You go in for an abscess on your face
and die in the MRI machine. The five or six
months left to you, you spend
crying and shaking uncontrollably
on linoleum, the hardwood loss
of hard work, your long and successful career
as a monster. Another woman comes
alive for the first time, kicking her dead frog
legs in a green pond at the heart of the forest.
Steak knives of electricity zigzag her left eye.
Winter sunrise crests over the shoulder
of a clay rabbit figurine so often mistaken
by actual rabbits as a sign of safe
passage that it has become one, a warmth
in the voice of the wind, steady lord over a fiefdom
of fool's gold oak leaves, bankrupt
currency in the land of rabid dogs. For her,
diagnosis equals wakeup call, Christmas
cookies, a chance to say goodbye or give a small piece
of her mind. It's the smell of clothes fresh
out of the drier, the feel of warm
water in the sponge, knuckles drooling with suds.

## Orange Lions

Shoveling the driveway the day before
my biannual MRI, I absorb the jolt of the handle.
When the head of my shovel catches

a crag of cracked cement and arrests
my movement, I remember how arduous shoveling
used to be as a boy, how I sank

the cutting edge again and again, getting
nowhere. There was always more dirty broken glass
to toss aside. The rough wet blocks

never felt completely clear of encrusted slush,
the incipient ice. At breakfast,
my 14-month-old feeds me the blackberries

Lili slices for him, keeping the banana
to himself. The orange lion heads
on his onesie stain yellow splotches of turmeric.

I try to understand the role of methylation
of the MGMT gene's promoter in my prognosis
but was never any good at science.

Because each footstep compacts the snow
into the denser translucency of ice, a dark archipelago
surfaces in the aisle between vehicles.

For the first time in my life, it feels good
to shovel. Because my son feeds me blackberries,
it feels good to suck the gritty halves

out of his grasp. Tomorrow Mom and I will
tunnel through I-70's dark bramble of snowy branches
and circle Arrowhead in search of the elusive gate.

Today hard snow tumbles in the dented tin I shove.
Behind me, a dark passage opens wide and clear.

## Carrot Cake

When you press in the bedroom dark
and whisper because our son is sleeping
your story of the long bus ride
to my 24th birthday party, the bakeries

you visited searching for a carrot cake
because I said it was my favorite, in Yantai
where there was no such thing,
and the baker who approximated one based

on your description of mine, I can almost glimpse
my 24-year-old self standing in the corner,
close-cropped and flushed, the unholy idiot,
wanton for want of experience.

How clumsily I maimed and married you.
I want to take him by the shoulders but they are only
my own. Tell me again how closely I spoke
with Sophia, the two of us leaning together like lovebirds,

while you hesitated, unsure of your status
in a drinking party, a pitstop for most
before the club, how you hesitated,
waiting to announce the cake I wouldn't even eat.

## Self-Portrait in an MRI Machine

For the hundredth time I lie down, listening
for the chirp of the coil chiller below McClean singing
*take me home, country roads* in my headphones.

The mirrors mounted overhead display me to myself
in three parts: the top mirror snags my bearded
chin, Mufasa-like and red, the mane

of a father at the height of his powers.
The bottom slat depicts the planetary top of my head,
shadowed outer rim, penumbra,

my left arm folded over my heart kicking like frog
legs on Luigi's dinner plate.
What the middle mirror shows are linens

draped over elevated knees, snowcaps drifting
farther and farther away,
as though an illusionist is sawing my body in half,

turning my lower half into a raft
that floats away while McClean sings *take me
home, take me home, take me home.*

## Travel Plans

Sky dark before dawn, the orange horizon an ashen log
left night long in the charcoal belly
of the firepit, the one bird that overwinters with me here,
the one nameless bird that whistles in the cold
the only song it knows, those same two notes— *you whoo.*

A white forest of frost grows on the front rail.
In the pines, a murder of crows explodes
into chorus, a black flurry
of wingbeats. If Monday's MRI comes back positive
for recurrence, how could I continue on
to Chicago? How catch my connecting flight?

In dreams, I leave my wallet in the glove
compartment, misplace my backpack on the shuttle
and scream all night long
for my passport, my boarding pass,
my year-old son. Little chapel drilled into pin oak bark,

whitewashed bird house, mini-sepulcher
complete with steeple and copper cross, what darkness you harbor
in your aperture, what inscrutable darkness
in your monocular inkblot. Where is your occupant, your sole
congregant and pastor of none?
Solitude becomes you because you disagree with everyone.

*international*

## The Long Flight Out of Myself

*Feb. 11, 2019*

I. The Flight

A man in hi-vis vest walks our taxiing behemoth.
He walks and waves us on. We ascend
through whiteout of raincloud, waterdrops
in the porthole spinning sideways. I close my eyes.

Falling, so aptly named, but not asleep,
I am falling back in time. My eyes roll back
in their sockets. I close my eyes,
teetering on the edge of infinite sleep.

Soaring west above the Arctic Ocean
in our windy cylinder, we switch on headlamps.
Soaring west, I walk through the black
spidery strands of complimentary earbuds.

Losing one ear and then the other,
I skip through buzzed-about movies I would not
otherwise
have chosen to see: silent films.

II. The City


Why is the smell essential? The body shop aroma
of Beijing winter air, tinge of cigarettes
loaded with garlic, the musk of our beefy driver,
a crewcut with which Lili confirms, Orchid
Garden Apartments, her college friend putting us up
for a week before the burial. This is the smell
I know of as China, a long-belated homecoming,
nearly five years since the seizure shipwrecked me
and Lili stateside. We arrive around nightfall.

Taxis jockey on the turnpike, swerving among pines,
pollards rung with guideposts. We arrive
during Spring Festival. The Year of the Pig,
deemed auspicious for the burial of my long dead
father-in-law. Hovering above a misty grid
of apartment blocks, bleak lots of winter
branches and weird bodies of water, we descend.

# First Day in Beijing

No time to write, I cannot find a moment
trying to keep my son alive, Lili and I heave Theo
into subway stations, those cold marble halls,
examine outdoor maps in February cleaver cold.
Escalators purr underfoot. Sliding doors slap
open and hiss shut. In order to register
myself and 16-month-old, I search the faces
of ten thousand human beings on the road
to a remote police station. Lili accosts
the kindhearted for mumbled directions.
Ten thousand human beings stare back at me.
Sidelong glances drop like shafts
about my strange little family, my adorable boy
strapped to what appears an ordinary Chinese
woman's chest. Ten thousand sidelong
glances and ten times that number of downcast
smartphone-illuminated gazes ghost me
and mine completely. On my first day in Beijing,
I am blessed with the poetry of only a little dirt
puffing between Theo's fingertips, the beauty
of the ash above us, its brown clumps of leaves
dangling outside China Unicom, a stack of chrome
window casements towering six stories tall.
His powdery pinch catches small gusts of wind.
How fortunate I feel for the dirt. Back in the store,
a lanky salesman with flat eyes is having trouble
shooting a photograph of my face. I stare into the black
lens, seated forever before his tall cheekbones,
his caved-in teeth, I peel off my spectacles again and again.
It seems to be a problem with the lens.

## Security Guards

I slink past the checkpoint
with my hood up, Old Summer Palace
West Road aglow, red lanterns

garlanding streetlights for the new year.
Beijing is a ghost town we're passing through
to meet a ghost. Our guardian angels

shuffle about their shining guard shack smoking
cigarettes in long overcoats,
fur hats, glass thermoses riverbed congested

with willow leaves. I encounter these red-embered
gatekeepers, these shapes of men trailing
clouds. Jetlagged bleary and baby-strapped in early

morning dark, I encounter these specters with KFC coffee
and croissant swinging from my wrist.
How strange it is to find myself living here, foreign as I am,

even to myself, but even an alien
has to sleep somewhere. Even a stranger has to eat.
Have mercy on me, brothers.

I married into your family.

## Orchid Garden Residence Community

Sunrise crests the sixth-story balconies. Bricks ridged
to guide the blind run down the middle of the sidewalk
into a cement pole. Miscellaneous mandarin orange peels,
sunflower seed shells, cigarette butts scatter underfoot.
Theo totters around the compound, picking them up
for the trash cans, hands ruddy in ice-bath wind.

Like my grandmother in Golden Acres who culled curbside
garbage on neighborhood walks, collecting bags
of walnuts for the basement, an elderly woman stirs about
in the shadows, sorting garbage.
When Theo approaches her dirty bucket, she shoos
his hands away.

Here by invitation, by the grace of an old friend, we pose,
globetrotters pretending to be Beijingers. The commissary boss
asks my nationality. We buy mulberries and quail eggs,
make believe. When afternoon light levels with the second story
window casements, grandmothers unpin clothes hung
between lamppost and tree trunk. Hedgerows harbor clumps
of snow like fugitives from the sun.

We visit the Summer Palace. Buy the obligatory map.
It says you're at the East Palace Gate, the Hall of Benevolence
and Longevity. It says Silver-Knuckled Wind, Theo
Hates the Harness with which you truss him.
Everyone admires his complexion. Smiles at the tantrums.

While Lili peruses the giftshops, Theo darts
about the Spacious Pavilion. Stopping just short
of the Seventeen-Arch Bridge, we call it quits.
Leave the wind to wisp in the yellow shoots of lakeside willows,
the magpies to cackle in their cypresses. We leave in favor
of an evening meal with friends, in favor of early bed.

Jetlagged and backpacked, we drag ourselves
back to Orchid Garden Residence Community
below a liver-spotted gibbous, the crackle of oil in the wok
of an upstairs apartment.

## KFC Rhapsody
*for Jordon Robert Shinn*


In five days I have fallen in love again
with the heavy-metal smell
of this necropolis. I have learned to drink
again from the wellspring
of secondhand smoke while Lili curses
and steps into the street.

On my last morning in Beijing
where five years earlier I contracted
myself to teach at the University
of the Chinese Academy of Sciences,
I take Old Summer Palace Road
to KFC for a final cup of freshly ground coffee.

Near the skywalk, a pair of eyes appears
pinched between hood and cowl
bloodshot in a slot of baked skin, scarves
hanging in long trains of filth
about an army green carapace of winter
coats, the orange vest of a sanitation worker.

Five years ago, I broke my contract.
On my last morning in Beijing, creosote
in the fireplace of the chalet

in Florissant, Colorado, where I first convulsed,
catches the house and its A-frame collapses
into an alphabet of ashes.

After I emailed my resignation,
friends raided my campus apartment, sifting
through the years Lili and I spent
at Beijing New Talent Academy. On my last day in Beijing
I meet Jordon at KFC for breakfast, who culled
through photos, scanned the contents

of hard drives, carried away rugs,
my guitar and Lili's essential oils, leaving
a mountain for the dumpster. On the walk back,
I wonder if the statue's moved,
the sightless seer, omen of my return,
ode to the city

that tried to eat me, the capitol
that stole my years. Because I'm still not likely
to live long, I wonder if the city's still
standing there with her back
to the wind, waiting
for me to pass.

## Last Flight Before the Burial

A misty jet whites out my porthole, deicing
the plated fin of the airbus sitting like a beached orca
on the tarmac, leaving the oblong lens
flecked and runny. We swivel into a straight shot
down the runway. The white ceiling
of our plastic cabin swings above us. Jouncing rubber
doughnuts give up the ground below.
While Theo strains to sit forward, I relax into freefall.

Shutters down, shafts of florescent light
brighten our dim cylinder of armchairs. Screens buzz
and unfold. Theo sprawls in my lap,
head flopped against my bicep. Lili's leans
into my shoulder blade. Behind me,
men hawk words like loogies. I feel the bird buoy
giddily in my seat. Its white noise, inside
of a vacuum cleaner roar, lulls us all.
Theo twitches. I adjust my hold.

Flight attendants in pink pantsuits bring dumplings.
Sun beats down melanomas on the steel flippers
of this aircraft that carries us living toward the dead man
who drank himself to death despite warnings
he was unable to heed, harkening to the earthen
jug of home-brewed rotgut in early morning,
dark devotee beside the cast-iron stove
where no one could say a word.
No one could complain.

## Tunnels

Riding out of Guiyang, we pass through a thousand tunnels.

Trundle into the dark intestines of mountain rock and blaze
out into sunlight. In lieu of daystar,
our headlights follow long planetary curves.

At regular intervals, fluorescents whisk over the dashboard,
scanning our bodies like the MRI machine that twice
annually xeroxes my brain.

Riding out of Guiyang, we hold our son between our knees.

No car seat, no seatbelts,
we trust in guardrails hovering high above the valley floor.
We hold our son.

Riding out of Guiyang, we roll past hillsides of headstones,
turretlike tombs, where the dead are held
in abeyance,

suspended in mid-air, like the man we have come to bury.

## Co-Sleeping

The only way it becomes possible for us to sleep him
with afternoon sun in the curtains is to lay
our bodies in the same bed. Even then he climbs
the headboard. Nowhere to go but up.

With my eyes closed, I listen for his breathing to drop
into a deep and regular pattern, for the faint
squeak of his binkie to stop. My mother-in-law Youqiong
describes sleeping at the right angles with Yilin

during his fourth and final illness, their heads touching
where the two wings met. Yilin fell several times
before he died. Swinging his legs over the edge,
he would land between sectional and coffee table.

I listen to the buses bellowing below our balcony window,
those giant caterpillars of plastic and glass crawling
past paint shops, toilets and light fixtures. Theo slaps my head.
Grabs Lili's hair. A tile saw squeals.

Farther off, passenger trains clatter over Nine Dragon Road.

Our boy finishes by playing with his own hands.
Quietly closes his eyes. At the end,
Yilin's entire family gathered. But it was only when a nephew
promised to take him home to Langdai that he went.

## Looking at the Courtyard

Because a mistake was made, explains
the fengshui master, Yilin's coffin
must be rotated by thirty degrees. If not,
someone in our family
is going to die. No one says me.
Everybody thinks it. Around suppertime,
an elderly woman in slippers pads
her dustpan to the dumpster.
A man sprouting white stubble in a black
leather flat cap shuffles
past one of China's pinched minivans, *loaf
of bread cars,* parked at the turquoise-tiled curb.

We all know he's taking advantage.
Around the gate, cattails tassel shopfront rooftops.
Theo shimmies the window screen
squeaking in its dirty track. Corn stalks,
wildflowers, even a small dark cherry
crowd the rooftops. Guizhou's spray-bottle
rain makes it possible for much
to be verdant. Because of my brain tumor,
I refuse rice. Decline corn and starchy
vegetables. Yilin's spider-cracked coffee table
I help a peasant woman distance
from the dumpster just sits there uncollected,
tarpaulin-draped below the pear tree.

## The Names of Children

I study the names of the children
who surround me—*Lin*

meaning forest. *Guo* meaning fruit.
The morose uncle with uremia

motions for me to sit beside the cast-iron
stove but I'm layered too thick

for burning coal. When sun gleams
for the first time since we arrive

in the milky tiles of the apartment block,
one blurry cloud like a smudge

on the lens, I hand over my pen
and Guo-Guo scratches out

a page in my knockoff Moleskine.
I write around her black, hairy

mass, increasingly banished
to the margins. Aunties ask what the hell

I'm doing. Lili explains, *collecting*
*material for poems.* Lin-Lin offers me a kernel

of candied popcorn. Aunties urge me
to try the tofu, beans and potato.

Lili explains, *cancer cells love glucose.*
Her aunts complain, *he can't eat anything.*

## Mother-in-Law

In rubber boots, Youqiong knees
the washing machine onto the balcony.
Most evenings she washes our clothes by hand

in front of the television, a plastic basin
between her feet, and hangs them above the cast-iron stove.
Most mornings I find the hot water heater already on

when I shuffle into the bathroom
because she beat me to the button. Theo discovers a shovel
on the balcony. He holds its rust-bitten head

in both hands, picks up a repurposed can
of pineapple juice and looks at mosquitos drowned
at the bottom as if he might lift the sawed off rim to his lips.

I pluck a pinwheel from a flowerpot and entertain him
briefly by blowing it into a blur. Youqiong wraps
the mouth of the spigot with silicone tape as a way of getting

the hose to attach. Tells me to get lost,
go back. Pouring the detergent in her palm, she swishes her hand
around in the churning water's wad of underwear and socks,

the sun-flowered blanket cover Theo peed on
in between diapers, his secondary sleep sack and onesie pajamas.
Afterwards, Theo and I grab handfuls of bubbles

from the diminishing mound of squishy foam. He runs them
to the makeshift bench and smears the board.
Again and again, he runs back for more

and the plank darkens
with his disintegrating handprints until Youqiong sees
and makes us stop.

## After the Revolution

Age 89, Lili's maternal grandfather
presses a copy of *Xi Jinping
Thought on Socialism With Chinese
Characteristics for a New Era*
into my hands. We draw our flight path
on his weathered world map.

The window behind him carries a little cloud
light into the musty room.
Whiskers of cigarette smoke graze his fur hat,
black overcoat of the man who served
a five-year a prison sentence
during the Cultural Revolution. Glasses of Oolong
curl above the potbellied stove.

Outside his little house, pinched
like a splinter between apartment blocks,
buses jostle onto Culture Road. Cheeks jiggle,
arm fat. Below mountain mist,
China's younger revolutionaries sashay,
sidestepping hawked loogies on smartphones.

Middle schoolers in tracksuits linger
over smoking grills and pineapple barrows.
Folding tables proffer sweaters, socks, leggings.
After the visit, our giant glass
rectangular fist slams into the market
bustle of boomboxes.

Food Fight

Theo's rice bowl drops
at the height of the argument

about him eating rice
when Youqiong calls Lili rigid

for refusing to serve him
rice and has her brother steam it

for him anyway. I airlift Theo
out of the room in his yellow frog

apron and green rubber bib,
crumb catcher still cradling

grains of the forbidden
starch he fills up on

to the exclusion of all else.
Later, Grandma's blood

smears the tile
where porcelain split

into white daggers she grasped,
jumping in with bare hands.

Uncle leaves his appetite
at the coffee table

after only a couple bites
of stir-fried celtuce, opting

instead to squat in the bedroom
with his tablet.

# Night Trains

Trains chatter over the arch
above Nine Dragon Road.

Lili whispers her father
began to see children

before he died, the fourth
and final time he fell ill.

They led him by the hand.
He tried to stab her ma

with a knife, she says.
Trains blow through the night,

wooing above the People's
Benefit apartments.

Yilin shattered the coffee table.
When Theo peels off

the plastic cover, I whisk him
to the bedroom. I wake up

and there's a shadow
on the balcony, darkening

the window curtains. Roosters
howl in the morning mist.

Massage Parlor


A man sitting on a stool feeds a bucket
full of flames at the corner of Welcome and Nine Dragon.
Our bus stalls outside the Second People's Hospital,
where Lili had herself examined using her mother's maiden name.

A red-scarfed woman cradles a pitcher of lemon water in her lap.
Schoolchildren scatter in red yellow tracksuits,
lovebirds. One has a wine-stained jawline.
The driver swings from his steering wheel behind a locked gate.

In my uncle's second wife's massage parlor, I am squeezed,
pounded, elbowed and kneed by my uncle's second wife.
Wallpaper of pink bouquets, easy listening.
On Construction Road, a burnt woman in a red apron

blowtorches a plucked chicken
in the face. A man lies upon a couch outside a shuttered shopfront,
three children jumping on his legs.
Black electrical wires spiderweb the cloudy sky,

pavement carpeted with sunflower seed shells. A girl toddler
crosses Construction Road to the doorstep, carrying
an almost whole apple with the skin eaten off.
She and Theo make eyes at each other through the crack

between plate glass doors. My uncle's second wife wears
a black overcoat with a gilded zipper. Her teeth are a train wreck.
She jerks my arm, snaps my fingers. By now the jumping
children have lain down with the man on the couch.

## Household Idol

Mounted above the doorframe, the Buddha
fills his tiny temple with pig-nosed corpulence.
He presides over my auntie's apartment.

By the red glow of two electric candles,
their wire threaded through a gash in the wallpaper,
he peels lips off bared teeth.

Five years ago, my auntie ran a mahjong table
clattering out of the backroom, gamblers
coming and going at all hours,

more or less in their money clips.
By the red glow, the two apples on his stoop spot
brown beside smoldering incense.

I'm not sure when the traffic stopped, only now
that my auntie's son is mayor, he is rarely
present at family dinners. His wife,

the schoolteacher in coke-bottle glasses,
buries her hands to the elbow in rubber gloves
while washing the dishes.

## In Search of Cherry Blossoms

Because our bus overshot the orchard,
we may not have descended through village heaps of rubble,
excretory garbage and stray dogs,
to the ocean valley's floor of cherry blossoms.

Because we missed the stop while I was practicing my rusty
Mandarin on a undergrad who had
questions for the American, we may never have reached
the vegetable garden hoed by a single woman

in an orange-striped sweater, sunbaked matron
picking her nose with pinkie finger,
or encountered her unabashedly staring son, growing green
onion above the white avalanche.

Deposited somewhere in Guizhou countryside, we may
have settled for the ghost town resort, the vacant
boulevard where a black sedan
is eternally stopped at the blinking crosswalk, a magpie

sails six empty lanes toward the pristine reception center,
and magnolia saplings with whitewashed trunks fritter away
creamy petals in hard February wind. Haunted by
somebody's moneyed vision of future profit,

we may—without glimpses of the shaggy
shanks of the thing itself—have mistaken a dream for reality.

## Offerings

Headshots of the dead parents backdrop a table
of offerings, a bucket of fried chicken,
a bowl of shrimp, red apples with brown spots.

It's not our apartment, so we steer away.
We steer Theo away from the space heaters,
the flat screen TV. Lin-Lin reappears
in her tutu, a knot on her forehead
Grandma dabs with pig fat, the boisterous
auntie with a Peter Pan haircut.

After dark, streetlights emblazon Naping Road
with Chinese lanterns, a stream of colors,
caravan of bright lights, cavalcade
stretching beyond this ancient kingdom
of high rises to another destination.

Dinner's cold by the time the last dish
hits the table, the last auntie arrives.
Baijiu warms the flushed uncles who sit long
getting drunk in a swirl of women
and children. By now they know not to offer me rice
wine—rice or wine, for that matter—not to risk
another lecture on cancer and ketosis.

By the end of the evening a bowl of strawberries
appears. Theo smears six or seven globs
of the sugary goop on his chin, his bib
and apron, by the time we realize our children
have eaten the offerings.

Visiting the Tomb

We travel seven thousand miles, ascend
into fog, the near total whiteout
of mountain mist, whisk

through blink-of-an-eye villages and resorts,
rag-dolling break-neck
passes above the unseeable valley floor.

Without seat belts, we hold our son
between our knees.
Yilin's tomb squats above terraced,

cow-pathed fields of rapeseed, and a flock
of white buildings, the village
in which Lili passed the first years of her life.

When the time comes, I thumb crumbly
yellow sheets of joss paper
and chuck them at a smoldering heap.

Lili tells me to pray for good fortune, good health.
We stop by a liquor store on the road
to the tomb and buy price spirits for the venerable

grandfather, the hated old man who introduced
a tender boy to the rotgut that would become as necessary
to him as the organs it corrodes.

## What Time Does

Cherry blossoms popcorn the hillsides
the last week of February.
Since my uncle first walked me to his gas station
pagoda, the hillsides have burst.

This is what time does. It tells you one thing,
then does another.
The first time I visited Six Bowls of Water,
I had no children.

Now I wear my son in a carrier. My shoulder
straps are always falling down.
The first time I visited, I had no diagnosis,
no timeframe. Now I walk around

with the tree of the knowledge of death in my head.
I don't always understand what my wife
is fighting with her mom about, hearing only
how tones harshen. Dinners shorten.

Even I begin to lose my appetite. Still,
it seems a shame to let such good pork ribs go to waste.

## Morning Departure

Roosters croak on the morning
of our departure. Youqiong wears her hair wet
in the new wrap, feet in rain

boots with drawstrings, an oriole perched
in chrysanthemums on the scroll
beside the door we close for the last time.

Only a few lights on in the window casements
on the morning of our departure,
only a few souls awake. Roosters hoarsen

in the gunmetal sky, taciturn mountain
streets, shopfront where Lili slurps her last bowl
of rice noodles in battery acid.

At the Six Plates of Water airport,
I hold Theo's hand and walk him down the stairs,
his two steps per stair equaling my one.

Reaching the bottom, we lurch between the up
escalator's rolling rubber handrails. I pull him
by the arm onto the step that lifts below us.

Again and again, we ride the escalator.
We run circles around the store
where shop girls stock shelves with bowls

of instant noodle, jars of pickled pepper.
Afterwards, I trade places with Lili and guard the carry-ons.
I take my seat among the waiting dead

who yawn at their smartphones and examine
boarding passes while Theo's screams resound
in the marble concourse.

## Terminal Destination

From a certain distance, the landscape is static,
alpine out the airplane window
bonsai, Zen.
So you focus on what's close up—the welter of footprints
in the wing's dirt or the book

in your hand.
From a certain distance, life is always on
pause, a still life.
Back up far enough and the people you know
don't even exist.

But step up close to these hills
and the green ridge
shows itself to be undulating, the stovepipe
in mid-puff.
A Chinese lantern tilts with the wind, its yellow tassels

waving as lightly as an anemone.
Step up close and know that you're here.
Your plane landed
a long time ago: terminal to concourse, concourse to taxi
stand, taxi home.

You've been living here a long time now
just to feel what it would be like,
just to know what the constellations would sound like
as finger positions
on the fret board in your hand.

**Cameron Morse** was diagnosed with a glioblastoma in 2014. With a 14.6 month life expectancy, he entered the Creative Writing program at the University of Missouri—Kansas City and, in 2018, graduated with an M.F.A. His poems have been published in numerous magazines, including *New Letters, Bridge Eight, Portland Review* and *South Dakota Review*. His first collection, *Fall Risk,* won Glass Lyre Press's 2018 Best Book Award. His second, *Father Me Again*, is available from Spartan Press and third, the chapbook *Coming Home with Cancer,* belongs to Blue Lyra Press's Delphi Poetry Series. He lives with his wife Lili and son Theodore in Blue Springs, Missouri, where he manages Inklings' FOURTH FRIDAYS READING SERIES with Eve Brackenbury and serves as poetry editor for *Harbor Review*.

This project was made possible, in part, by generous support from the Osage Arts Community.

Osage Arts Community provides temporary time, space and support for the creation of new artistic works in a retreat format, serving creative people of all kinds — visual artists, composers, poets, fiction and nonfiction writers. Located on a 152-acre farm in an isolated rural mountainside setting in Central Missouri and bordered by ¾ of a mile of the Gasconade River, OAC provides residencies to those working alone, as well as welcoming collaborative teams, offering living space and workspace in a country environment to emerging and mid-career artists. For more information, visit us at www.osageac.org

www.ingramcontent.com/pod-product-compliance
Lightning Source LLC
Chambersburg PA
CBHW030131100526
44591CB00009B/605